CW01020769

SCRIVENER - PURE AND SIMPLE

A simple, no-nonsense guide to working with Scrivener for
the first time.

By
Gerald Hornsby

COPYRIGHT

First Published 2017

Hard Pressed Books
www.hardpressedbooks.com

ABOUT THE AUTHOR

Gerald Hornsby began writing seriously in 2003. Despite working full time and with a family, he began pounding keys into the early hours, striving to become a literary short story writer.

That didn't work.

But some lessons were learnt, and as he stepped across the border into genre and longer fiction, he attempted to bring some of that literary experience with him.

Enough of the third-person stuff.. Yeah, this is me. I am a Scrivener fan, but only because I found a way of working with it which hid most of the frills and fancy bits which I found confusing. I wanted a simple system which actually helped me write my fiction, and didn't get in the way.

Scrivener for me is that system. I hope that, by sharing this short book with you, it will be your system too.

INTRODUCTION

What is Scrivener?

Put simply, Scrivener is a word processor invented for writers. Yes, it allows you to type words into a document, like all word processors. But Scrivener is a bit more than that. The creators have built-in a number of features which aid authors, which allow them to create a smoother workflow. My own experience is that is a lot more reliable than, say, 'other' word processors on the market.

"All very well, Gerald," you say, "but I know my own favourite, and I've done lots of writing on it, and it works pretty well, and you're not selling Scrivener to me."

Indeed, I'm not. That's not my job. But ...

Scrivener is a system which allows me to keep EVERYTHING about my novel, short story, non-fiction piece, whatever, IN ONE PLACE. In its single file, you can have your words, your research, photos of locations and of actors cast in the role of your characters. It allows you to create multiple versions of your writing from one set of text documents. PDF, docx, Mobi, ebook, markdown ... you name it, it will produce it. Also, its structure allows for automated production of different versions of your work. Update your writing, and all published versions can be changed and updated, automatically.

Still not enough?

It has a corkboard system which can be used when planning your writing. It allows scenes or chapters to be moved around the manuscript with impunity.

Joanna Penn gives 3 reasons for using Scrivener:

1) You can write in scenes, and drag and drop to re-order

2) You can auto-create Kindle and epub files

3) Project binders can also hold notes, research, pictures and more, so you have one place for the whole ecosystem of your book.

Pretty good. If you search online for "Reasons to use Scrivener", you'll find many authors listing the features they find useful and / or essential.

However, the thing has about a thousand different options for a thousand different features, and for some, this is the main stumbling block. Man, is this software over-complicated for new users. Which is where this book comes in. I've lost count of the number of times I've spoken about Scrivener, showing new users why, actually, it's pretty simple to get up and running. And, after reading this book, you will know, too.

A bit of history

I first came across Scrivener in 2010, and actually bought it in 2011. And yet, it was several years before I began to use it? Why? Because it looked so damned complicated. I was overawed by the plethora of options and features. I just wanted to type words!

Despite working with computers since the time my employer had one computer, kept in a sealed room and tended by technicians in white coats, I'm a bit of a Luddite. I don't like over-complication, and I used to think that writing was simply about putting letters together to make words, and getting them into a computer by the simplest possible means. Microsoft Word is an ugly behemoth. Simple editors don't have word count facility. So for a long time, I used a free program called Bean. Here it is:

http://www.bean-osx.com/Bean.html

It did everything I needed it to do - it loaded quickly, worked reliably, and I used it all the time for writing. I still use it today for single file writing, letters, simple stuff. If you're looking for something straightforward that just works, check it out. It's solid and works on all Intel Macs running OS X up to El Capitan.

And then I heard about this wonderful thing called Scrivener. I looked at the screenshots. "My, that looks complicated," I thought. "All I want to do is have the buttons I press on the keyboard bring letters on the screen."

Eventually, the pressure became too great, and I downloaded the trial version.

(NB: The trial version is the same as the paid-for version, but time-limited to 30 days. But this is a real '30 days of use' days, not 30 calendar days from the first time you open it. So you can use it for 5 days this year, and it will still give you 25 days of use next year).

I opened it up on the sample document. "My, this looks really complicated," I said, and after a few minutes looking and clicking, I closed it again. "I'll look at it when I have more time."

Of course, this "more time" construct is a myth. You and I will never have "more time". But I kept hearing that people loved it, and said things like "I don't know how I worked before Scrivener". So I looked at it again. And closed it again. "I don't need all that complication".

Some time later, I used my 50% discount code from NaNoWriMo to register (buy) the thing. I think I paid around £15. "It'll be useful sometime," I said to myself.

Fast forward ... a bit. I don't know how long it was. Probably a year or two. And there I was, happily writing my latest masterpiece, chapter by chapter, in good old Bean. Each chapter a different file, incrementing file names for each time I saved (see the later chapter "Backing Up" for my (almost) failsafe regime.

And then …

Uh-oh. I need to add a new chapter in the middle of what I've written so far. Which means all the chapter numbering was wrong, and all the file names would be wrong (nowadays, I'm older and wiser, and would write the chapter and call it "Chapter Two-a" or something, and carry on writing).

This coincided with a growing interest in scriptwriting. Not for writing scripts, you understand, but to help me with story structure. And I had an epiphany - "I SHALL WRITE IN SCENES, AND USE SCRIVENER!"

And, to be honest, I haven't look back since (yes, I'm one of those annoying people). I opened Scrivener to the sample document, took out everything I didn't need, and there it was. MY version of Scrivener.

WHY THIS BOOK?

There are many, many books and workshops and videos and instructional texts about Scrivener. Many, many, many. I know. I've looked at a lot of them. But most of them spend their time telling us how 'feature-rich' Scrivener is - it can do this, and it can do that, and there's something else it can do.

Since I've become a regular Scrivener user, I've tried to spread the word. I've written a couple of blog posts about why I became a Scrivener Devotee, and how I finally understood how to use it that made sense to me.

Whenever someone has asked me about it, I've highlighted that most of the help for Scrivener is written from a technical standpoint. Even the accomplished author David Hewson, who was an early devotee, and who wrote a "How to write a novel in Scrivener" book, threw features at the reader.

That's not how to help people who can't see the wood for the trees; who get swamped by a deluge of features and menus and buttons. "I just want to enter some words". Even the Ugly Behemoth itself (MS Word) starts with a blank document, and a flashing cursor, and you press a letter key, and up it pops on the screen.

The intention of this book is just to get you started using Scrivener. You can explore advanced features later on if you want to. In the 'wood for the trees' analogy, I'm showing you the wide and straight path through the forest, and even holding the gate open for you.

SCREEN LAYOUT

Most word processors open with a blank screen, or a blank page, simulating a piece of paper. And you begin to write.

Not so for Mister Scrivener. You open him up, and you get a crazy, complicated splurge of boxes and windows and buttons and symbols and ... a screenful of confusion. There are things all over the screen, and you don't know where to click first. And it is this, along with some peculiar naming conventions, that causes newcomers to the software many difficulties.

Let's begin by starting up Scrivener, shall we? Or, if you're already looking at it, start a new project from the File menu. You'll be offered a choice of templates. A template is a way of setting up a general-purpose program to work best for a particular use.

And a quick note - all screenshots are from the current (October 2017) Mac OS X version. The Windows version may have slight differences.

The Template chooser looks like this:

Input

File → Input → File select files

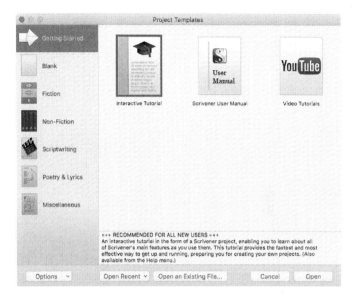

STAY AWAY FROM THE GETTING STARTED SECTION! Seriously.

Sorry to shout, but that way lies sadness and frustration. Choose the next one down - "Blank". It'll ask you what you want to call the project. You can rename it later, so just call it TESTING for now. Or call it whatever you like.

Your screen should look a bit, or quite a lot, like the picture below:

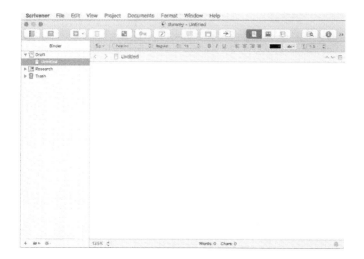

Ignore all the icons and buttons and options. You could, if you want, just begin typing in the centre pane right now. Hey presto! You're using Scrivener to write!

But before that, let's start with the biggest, stupidest naming convention, shall we? The Binder.

When you think about it, technically, the Binder is a pretty good name for something which is, essentially, a collection of documents. My problem is that I bind something when it's complete, and finished. Scrivener's binder is either full of a mass of different ... *stuff*, if you open the sample project, or nothing, if you open the <blank> project.

I would have preferred it be called something like the Filing Cabinet, because that's where you store things like writing, research, mood boards, casting outlines, notes, location photographs, empty crisp packets.

So, this thing on the left is where everything about your project is stored. EVERYTHING. And this is the content of the single project file that Scrivener produces.

There is a fairly standard menu bar across the top, like most pieces of software, and there are some common options represented graphically underneath. Don't worry about those for the moment.

And in the middle - is the work area. Most of the time, this displays your text, your photos, whatever you've clicked on in the binder ... err ... filing cabinet. It's like you open a drawer in the cabinet, and you can see what's inside.

And that's about it for now. There. It wasn't that bad, was it? Just remember:

BINDER = PROJECT FILING CABINET

ORGANISING YOUR BINDER

So, as writers, what do we need to do? Apart from procrastinate, drink coffee and eat cake.

We need to enter words into a document.

Documents can go anywhere in the filing cabinet (binder). But you wouldn't want to spread them around in random drawers, would you?

Answer: No, Gerald, we wouldn't.

Because that would be stupid. You wouldn't know where to look for them when you needed them next. And you don't just drop pieces of paper in the bottom of a drawer, do you?

Answer: No, Gerald. That would be very stupid.

So, what's the first stage? You need to create a document in the binder. When you start a new project, you should have a document called "Untitled" in your "Draft" folder. So you can use that, if you want. Or you can create a brand-new shiny one, all of your own. Don't worry, it doesn't hurt. Right-click on "Draft" and select "Add" and then select "New Text". You'll get an "Untitled" document, but highlighted. Type in your title for this document. You can it "Scene One" or "Chapter One" or "Testing" or whatever you jolly well like. You'll see the document title in your binder, and you can go right ahead now and being typing words in the central pane on the screen.

Now repeat, until you've written a book. See? I told you it was easy.

Of course, if you only have a few documents, you can do it this way. Here's part of the binder for a project I'm working on - a beginners' guide to Scrivener. I know, using screenshots from a project within a project could make the software explode. But it doesn't.

My manuscript only has eight chapters at the time of writing, so they're all lying in the bottom of the 'Manuscript' drawer. That's okay. There are only eight documents, and we can sift through to find the right one.

Here's a screenshot of another project - this is my annual project to write a short story a week. Sadly, falling behind this year, but you get the idea:

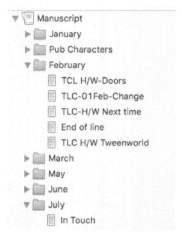

In the screenshot above, you can see I have folders (think of them as hanging files) so the five shorts I wrote in February are in a separate hanging file (folder) called, strangely, "February". You can go to the "Project" menu option, and click on "Add folder" or "Add document". Easy peasy. When you highlight a document, begin typing into the large pane in the middle. You're writing!

Of course, you could make folders for book sections, with a document for each chapter.

Here's another example:

I'm using an 8-part structure, with scenes as individual documents in each part. Wondering about the little green flags? Don't. It's not important now.

TEXT ENTRY

You can now begin typing away in the centre pane, adding words to your manuscript, crafting stories and articles and ... well, anything really. You now know how to organise your binder to make it look how you want, and how it makes most sense to you.

You can change the size of the font easily:

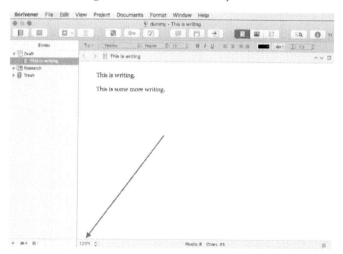

So now, you can write and write until the writing's done.

There is one other trick - and that is the feature which blanks out the rest of your screen. We writers are easily distracted, and even though we may be concentrating on our work, if there's a window open in the background with a flashing message, we are likely to switch to that other window.

Cmd-Alt-f changes that for you, and fades everything else on your screen to somewhere between transparent to black.

This is now all getting a bit meta, where I'm using this book as an example to use in ... this book. Before I disappear into my own orifice, let's move on to what we do when we've finished writing our masterpiece.

COMPILE / EXPORT

Arrgghh! We're back to obscure naming conventions again.

This time we're talking about the Compile feature. For those who have knowledge of writing software, compiling is what you do to convert plain text instructions into machine language that a computer can understand. And you can see what's going on here. Scrivener will take your plain text (in the form of your story) and convert it into something an ebook reader can understand. Or a PDF file reader. Or another program, like Microsft Word. So, maybe the creators of Scrivener are *technically* correct. Your words are just your words, but the final document formatting is all done in Compile.

But compiling is not the word that most of the rest of humanity uses for this process. Most of us now call this "Exporting". You export stuff (writing) from one program to another. Which is also a good, technical description.

SO WHY NOT CALL IT EXPORT INSTEAD OF COMPILE?

Having got that off my chest, the Compile function has a number of handy presets which allow you to quickly get from one format to another. One I use a lot is the PDF creator. Although you can print direct from Scrivener, sometimes it's nice to be able to send or print a PDF file. Recently, a friend wanted to see some examples of flash fiction. I opened my "Short story a week" Scrivener file from last year, and highlighted a few stories from the Binder (grrr) and Compiled them to a PDF file which I was able to send to my friend within

30 seconds of opening Scrivener. Doing something like that with Microsoft Word frightens me to death. Scrivener 1 - Word 0.

Of course, Scrivener Compile being created by the people that wrote Scrivener, it has about fifty million different options, and even beginning to scratch the surface of those options is way beyond the scope of this book.

As described above, you can select the complete manuscript, or parts thereof, or just one chapter or a group of scenes to Compile.

Here's a screenshot (meta again) of me wanting to produce a (small) PDF of just this section of the book:

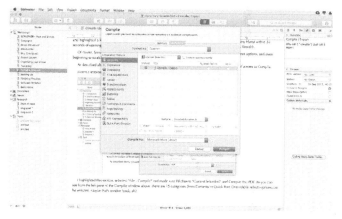

I highlighted this section, selected "File - Compile" and made sure I'd chosen "Current Selection" and Compile for: PDF. As you can see from the left pane of the Compile window above, there are 15 categories (from Contents to Quick Font Override) in which options can be selected. Maybe that's another book, eh?

BACKING UP

Technology can, and does, go wrong. Even if it doesn't go wrong, you can spill liquids on your computer (don't ask me how I know), a small child can drop it or a furry pet can jump on it and destroy it. Or even, a nasty person can break into your house and steal it. Or you can leave it on a bench in the middle of Germany (again, don't ask me how I know).

How much is your work worth? Say, you've written 100,000 words at around 500 words an hour (which includes planning time and staring out of the window time). That's 200 hours work, MINIMUM. At minimum wage, that's £1,500. And that's a minimum. It's more likely to be double that or more for a completed manuscript. And yet, you mean to tell me, you only have ONE COPY of that in the whole wide world?

That's not very clever.

This is what I do. You don't have to do this. You might have other methods of safeguarding your work. But my security protocol (sounds posh, eh?) consists of two layers - file naming, and physical storage.

PROTOCOL ONE
Going all meta again, these are the current files I have for this project:

Scriv Non Fic-001.scriv
Scriv Non Fic-002.scriv
Scriv Non Fic-003.scriv
Scriv Non Fic-004.scriv
Scriv Non Fic-005.scriv
Scriv Non Fic-006.scriv

Notice anything?
Here's the files for another project:

Circles of Corruption.026.scriv
Circles of Corruption.025.scriv
Circles of Corruption.025.pdf
Circles of Corruption.024.scriv
Circles of Corruption.023.scriv
Circles of Corruption.022.scriv
Circles of Corruption.021.scriv
Circles of Corruption.020.scriv
Circles of Corruption.019.scriv
Circles of Corruption.018.scriv

That one has a PDF file sneaked in there. But the key thing is that there are multiple copies of the project, with an incrementing numerical suffix.

So here's what I do:

The first time I create a new project, I call it "**2017-Project-001**" or something like. The key thing here is the '-001'. Then, after a couple of hours' work, or maybe a day, I perform a "Save As …" command, and call the new file "**2017-Project-002**". I now have an updated copy of my work, saved to a physically new file. The old one is still there.

I continue doing this. When the first draft of something is complete, I call it something like "**2017-Project-FD-001**". Edits end up in more sequentially-numbered filenames.

"Gerald," you say, "that's rather a lot of work. And doesn't it take up valuable disk space?"

Answer: No, and No.

1. It takes around 5 seconds, maybe less, to save under a new filename. Is safeguarding your work worth five seconds a day? Is your time so valuable you can't afford five seconds?

2. A 50,000 word manuscript, with planning and research and ideas and so on takes up around one megabyte of disk space. You can have 1,000 versions of this to take up one gigabyte. Many laptops now have terabytes of disk space. If you're really worried, you can delete the older versions of the files, if you so wish. My complete "2016-writing" folder is less than a gigabyte, and it has sequential files of my 'write a short story a week' challenge (over 60 of them), first drafts (multiple files) of two novellas, incomplete first drafts (multiple files) of 2 longer works, plus spreadsheets and planning and research and ideas and … and …

I think you get the picture.

PROTOCOL TWO

Hard disks fail. Yes, they do. To believe otherwise is just plain stupid. Sorry if that offends, but it's true.

I came to computing when data was entered on a long string of paper tape. My first disk drives took eight-inch floppy disks, that had a capacity of around 100kbytes (that's a tenth of a megabyte), and the disk would last a week (if you were lucky) before they failed. And they really were floppy.

So I have an inbuilt mistrust of data storage devices. Call me old-fashioned, but I like to have copies of my valuable data in more than one place. Again, this is not an onerous protocol. You just have to get used to doing it.

A) The easiest thing to do is to email the file to yourself once a week. Next time you're checking your email, send an email to yourself, and attach your latest Scrivener file. Job done!

B) Use USB 'thumb' sticks. These are huge nowadays for very little money. £10 will buy you 32GB of safe storage. Tell you what - buy two. Alternate between them. I back up the files I'm working on (sometimes the whole of a project folder) at least once per week.

C) Use external USB hard disks. These are relatively cheap now. I can buy a 2TB (terabyte) external drive for less than £50. And a good one, at that. You can afford to back up your whole writing folder whilst you're having lunch or something. And, while you're investing in security, buy a second USB hard disk, too. Alternate big backups, but give one to a neighbour. Theft or fire could destroy your precious backups.

PROTOCOL X - Scrivener auto-backup.

Yes, there is an automatic backup that can be configured, and you can choose how often you want Scrivener to back up its work files. Here are the options on a Mac:

There are lots of different options you can choose.

BUT - there is a key thing here. For me, the auto-backup is an option of last resort. I will only go to this if there has been a serious mess-up with my normal backup files. Scrivener backup will overwrite older files. If something's been lost for a long time, the last good backup may have been overwritten. You can't go back indefinitely.

REMEMBER:
1) Use incrementing "Save As ..." file names.
2) Email your latest file to yourself once a day.
3) Backup your writing files to alternate USB sticks at least once per week.
4) Backup your writing folder to USB hard disk at least once per month.

FINISHING TOUCHES

Having written your story, and having read it, edited it, re-read it, re-edited it, shown it to beta readers, re-edited it, polished it, copyedited it, proofread it, and finally … edited it, it's ready to go on sale.

As I said before, Scrivener has a number of acceptable formats for ebook and print book publishing, but you can't just take your words from your manuscript and publish them.

"Why not, Gerald?"

Because a manuscript does not a published novel make. You will need to add some, or all, of the following:

Front matter - this is Cover artwork, title page, copyright, dedication (if applicable), introduction (if applicable), contents page, and acknowledgements (if applicable)

Back matter - e.g. Call to action, request reviews, links to other books, links to author website, offer to join email list, links to other books, about the author (including web links and social media links).

Each part of the front and back matter takes the form of a text document, exactly as your scenes / chapters are in the manuscript. These can then be included / excluded from the compile function when you produce your finished novel.

Another feature to quickly mention is Collections. This allows you to have one copy of your text, but differing versions of front and back matter. Look it up when you feel ready to dive in.

There is a plethora of options for you to choose from, which can enhance the visual appearance of your novel, but these are way beyond the scope of this introductory guide. If you want to frighten yourself, search for ***advanced formatting scrivener*** and look at some of the links that crop up.

BUT NOT NOW!

As with much of Scrivener, you can spend hours and days and weeks exploring all of its many options, but is it all worth it? What's more important - that your novel includes a fancy graphic at the beginning of each chapter, or that you get your book finished and produced and you move on to create the next one? It's the latter, of course.

BELLS AND WHISTLES

This final chapter is to highlight, briefly, some of the extra features that the designers have built in to Scrivener. These are features that go beyond the requirements for text entry and output formatting and so on. This is not an exhaustive list, nor is it a guide to show you how to use them. This book is to get you using Scrivener for the first time, to demystify the complexity of the program, and to help you write your next prize-winning novel!

Sample character names.

Finding that right name for your character is a key decision for any author. The name needs to reflect the character in some way, and you might need it to be a common name, or an uncommon name. Scrivener to the rescue! You can choose male, female, both. You can include or exclude different nationalities, obscurity level, and so much more. It's a great feature.

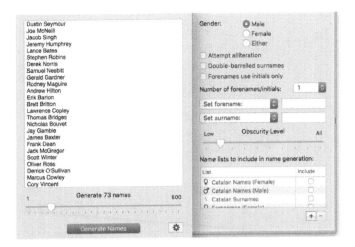

Auto backup.

As mentioned in the "Backing Up" chapter, Scrivener includes an auto backup procedure, where on a timed basis, it will save your file for you. This is not stored in your work folder, but in a separate backup folder. For me, as already explained, this is for DISASTER RECOVERY ONLY. The backup overwrites previous backups on an oldest-first basis, so the particular version you might be looking for could have already been overwritten.

Targets / word count.

I don't personally use this feature, but since Scrivener counts your words for you as you're typing, it gives you the ability to set a target number of words to type per day or session.

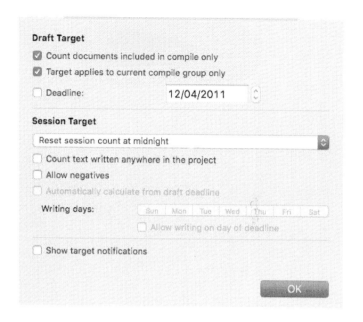

Corkboard.

Scrivener can simulate a corkboard / index card layout for when you're planning your novel. Again, I don't use this feature.

This is what the corkboard looks like for this book:

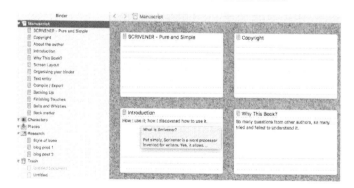

Very pretty, if you like that sort of thing. Moving the cards around has the effect of changing the order of the documents in the binder.

And that finished this short book on Beginning Scrivener. I hope you found it useful, and that it's helped you take those first tentative steps into this amazing piece of writing software.

As I said earlier, I wouldn't contemplate beginning a new writing project in anything but Scrivener now. I hope that, one day, you'll feel the same.

THE END

If you have enjoyed this book, please sign up to the Hard Pressed Books newsletter, at
http://hardpressedbooks.com/newsletter/
And please browse the other books from the same publisher.

Printed in Great Britain
by Amazon

49584318R00020